Sorting

SORTING Money

by Jennifer L. Marks

Capstone press

Mankato, Minnesota

A+ Books are published by Capstone Press,
151 Good Counsel Drive, P.O. Box 669, Mankato, Minnesota 56002.
www.capstonepress.com

1 2 3 4 5 6 12 11 10 09 08 07

Library of Congress Cataloging-in-Publication Data
Marks, Jennifer L.
    Sorting money / by Jennifer L. Marks.
    p. cm.—(A+ books. Sorting)
    Summary: "Simple text and color photographs introduce basic concepts of sorting
money"—Provided by publisher.
    Includes bibliographical references and index.
    ISBN-13: 978-0-7368-6738-2 (hardcover)
    ISBN-10: 0-7368-6738-4 (hardcover)
    ISBN-13: 978-0-7368-7856-2 (softcover pbk.)
    ISBN-10: 0-7368-7856-4 (softcover pbk.)
    1. Counting—Juvenile literature. 2. Money—Juvenile literature. I. Title. II. Series.
QA113.M37 2007
513—dc22
                                                 2006017361

Credits

Ted Williams, designer; Charlene Deyle, photo researcher; Scott Thoms, photo editor;
    Kelly Garvin, photo stylist

Photo Credits

American Numismatic Association Money Museum, 29 (top)
BigStockPhoto.com/Christy Thompson, 27 (top)
Capstone Press/Karon Dubke, cover, 2–3, 4, 5, 6, 7, 8, 9, 10–11, 12–13, 14–15, 16–17, 18–19,
    20–21, 22–23, 24, 25, 28
iStockphoto Inc./Dane Wirtzfeld, 29 (bottom)
PhotoEdit Inc./Cindy Charles, 26
SuperStock/Dwight Ellefsen, 27 (bottom)

Note to Parents, Teachers, and Librarians

The Sorting set uses color photographs and a nonfiction format to introduce readers to the key math skill of sorting. *Sorting Money* is designed to be read aloud to a pre-reader, or to be read independently by an early reader. Images and activities encourage mathematical thinking in early readers and listeners. The book encourages further learning by including the following sections: Table of Contents, Facts about Money, Glossary, Read More, Internet Sites, and Index. Early readers may need assistance using these features.

Table of Contents

Money, Money, Money!

Look at all the loot! Lemonade stands are a great way to make some summer spending money.

4

But now what? Sorting can help you see what money you have and how much it's worth.

Pennies, quarters, nickels, and dimes! Each kind of coin looks a little different.

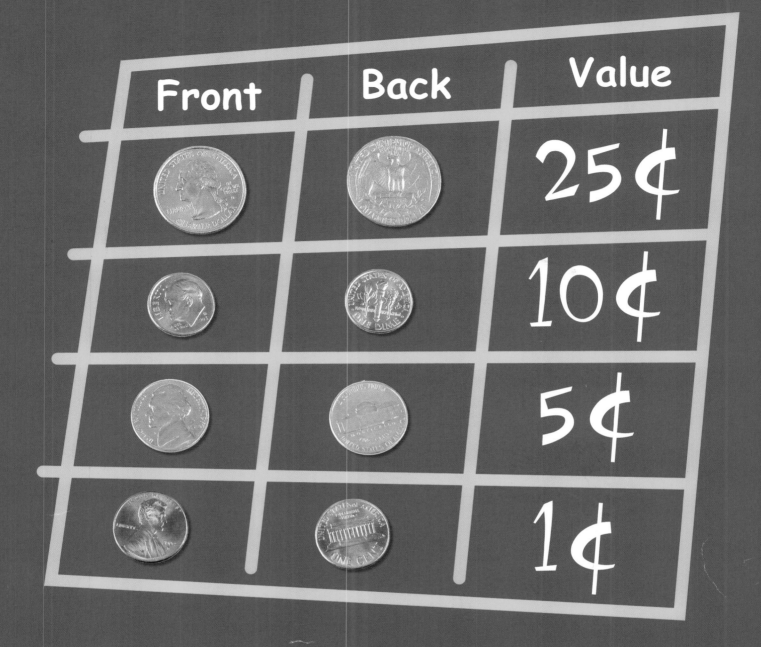

Front	Back	Value
		25¢
		10¢
		5¢
		1¢

Here's the real size of the coins, front and back. Do you know what each one is worth? A lowercase c with a line through it stands for "cents."

Dollar bills are money that's printed on paper.

8

A one dollar bill is worth
100 cents. Do you know whose
face is on this bill? George
Washington, the first president,
is the one.

Sort It Out

You can sort money by grouping the same kinds of coins together—quarters, dimes, nickels, pennies.

You can sort by color too. Pile all the copper coins together. Copper is a color, and it's the name of a metal used to make pennies.

Sort all the silver
coins into another pile.

Run your finger over the skinny edge of a coin. Does it feel bumpy or smooth?

These coins are sorted
into sets with bumpy
or smooth edges.

Coins can be sorted by size too. Try sorting smallest to biggest.

Dimes are the smallest and quarters are the biggest. What comes in between?

Money can be sorted by value,
or how much it's worth.

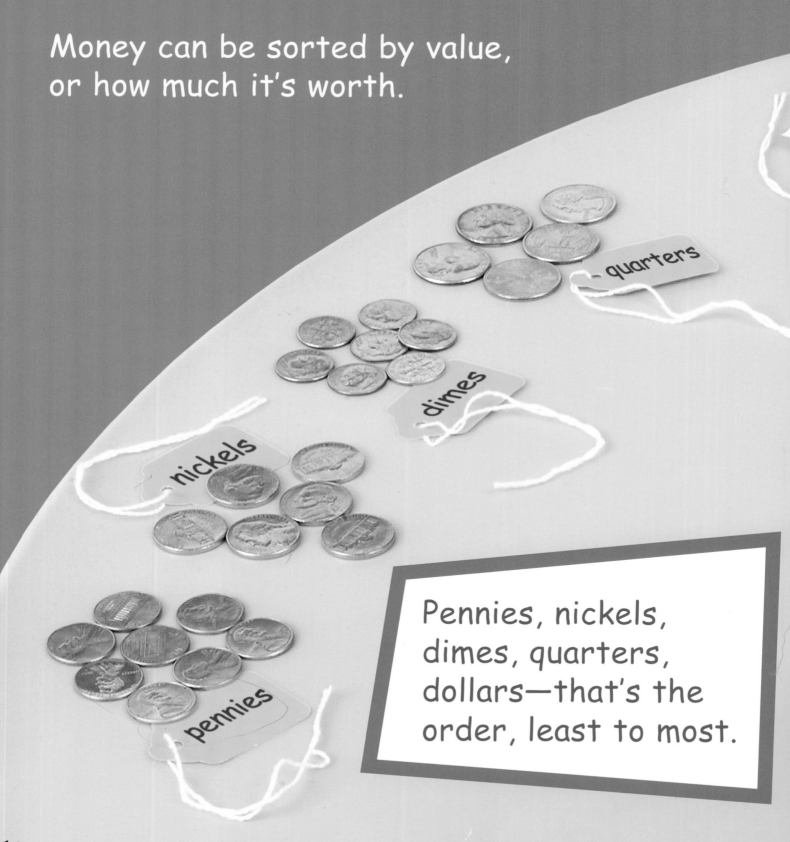

quarters

dimes

nickels

pennies

Pennies, nickels,
dimes, quarters,
dollars—that's the
order, least to most.

quarters

dollars

Let's try that backward! From dollars down to pennies, this money is sorted from greatest value to least.

dimes

nickels

pennies

You can sort coins to make 5¢, 10¢, and 25¢. Use just one coin or use a few.

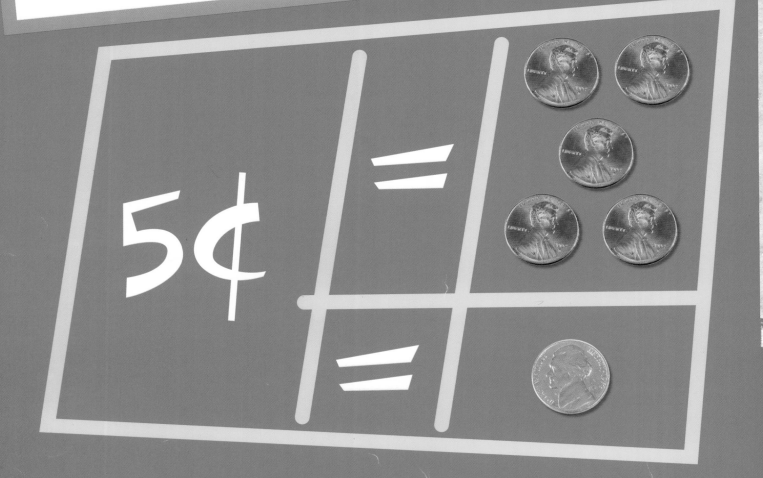

5¢ =

22

10¢ =

25¢ =

23

Make a Dollar

No matter how you sort it, a dollar always equals 100 cents. You can make a dollar in many different ways.

This is a dollar.

This is a dollar.

This is a dollar.

Sorting Money in the Real World

You can spot sorting in all kinds of places. Let's look at some ways people sort money in the real world.

Some people collect coins. They use special books to sort their coins by age, mint, state, or other traits.

Cashiers use cash registers to sort and count money. The money is sorted and kept in the register's drawer.

Banks use machines to sort coins for them. Bank workers dump the coins in, and the machine separates each kind of coin.

Facts about Money

■ Coins start out as blank circles. The blank coins are pickled, or soaked in a special mixture to make them clean and shiny. Powerful machines stamp images onto the coins. This process is called pressing.

■ A place that presses coins is called a mint. There are four American mint locations. They make all of the United States' coins and some coins for other countries too.

■ You've seen dollar bills, but did you know that there are dollar coins too? The newest dollar coin is called the Golden Dollar. It is a yellowish color and features Sacagawea and her baby.

- The first American coins were created in the fall of 1792. They were worth five cents and were called half-dimes or dismes.

- For many years, most American coins were made from gold and silver. Now they are made out of other less-expensive metals.

- The average dollar bill wears out after about 1 ½ years. Coins, on the other hand, last for about 30 years.

- According to legend, the United States' first coins were made out of silverware donated by the first lady, Martha Washington.

- The backside of the buffalo-nickel coin shows an American bison. Many claim that the bison shown was a real animal named Black Diamond from the New York Central Park Zoo.

Glossary

bill (BIL)—a piece of paper printed with a design and used as money

cent (SENT)—a unit of money; 100 cents are equal to one U.S. dollar.

coin (KOIN)—a small piece of metal stamped with a design and used as money

dollar (DOL-ur)—the main unit of money; one U.S. dollar is equal to 100 cents.

set (SET)—a group of things that go together

sort (SORT)—to arrange or separate things into groups

value (VAL-yoo)—the amount that something is worth; each kind of coin has a different value.

Read More

Pistoia, Sara. *Money*. MathBooks. Chanhassen, Minn.: Child's World, 2006.

Pluckrose, Henry Arthur. *Sorting and Sets*. Let's Explore. North Mankato, Minn.: Sea to Sea, 2006.

Thayer, Tanya. *Counting Money*. First Step Nonfiction. Minneapolis: Lerner, 2002.

Internet Sites

FactHound offers a safe, fun way to find Internet sites related to this book. All of the sites on FactHound have been researched by our staff.

Here's how:

1. Visit *www.facthound.com*

2. Choose your grade level.

3. Type in this book ID **0736867384** for age-appropriate sites. You may also browse subjects by clicking on letters, or by clicking on pictures and words.

4. Click on the **Fetch It** button.

FactHound will fetch the best sites for you!

Index